Sunfish Sailing

A QUICK & EASY GUIDE

CHAILLE & LARRY KELLY

E P B M

ECHO POINT BOOKS & MEDIA, LLC

Published by Echo Point Books & Media
Brattleboro, Vermont
www.EchoPointBooks.com

Copyright © 1961, 2015 Chaille and Larry Kelly

ISBN: 978-1-62654-856-5

Illustrations by Lt. Cdr. Kieran Kilday U.S.N.R.

Editorial and proofreading assistance by Christine Schultz,
Echo Point Books & Media

Printed and bound in the United States of America

TABLE OF CONTENTS

SAIL HO!

Sailfish and Sunfish have provided us with many glorious hours of pleasure on summer afternoons with our friends and their families. Whether in a race for a trophy or sailing just for fun, it is always a thrill to be aboard these delightful craft.

Before an afternoon is over, everyone from the very youngest to the very saltiest will have skippered his boat and shared in the recap of the day's excitement. This is the unique pleasure of Sailfish and Sunfish—they can

be enjoyed by the whole family. On these precisely designed boats a seven year old can learn the basics of sailing, wind and water. As well, his parents can derive great excitement from racing over a two mile course.

The simplicity of the boats is a primary appeal and asset. They are truly slaves to their owners since they are easily transportable, quickly assembled for the water and economically stored.

In this booklet we hope to impart the pleasure of our Sailfish and Sunfish experiences and to acquaint you with the basic fundamentals of sailing and racing these boats.

WHO · WHAT · WHERE

WHO? *Swimmers of any age are candidates for Sailfish and Sunfish skippers:* A skipper with or without a crew of one can handle his agile craft with ease, since managing the tiller[*] and single sail is all that is required. A child who is trained in the rules of safety and sailing may well be a worthy challenger for "first around the marker" in competition with his father!

[*]See Glossary for definition of all terms.

- WHEN - WHY?

WHAT?

A Sailfish or Sunfish is what you make it. A water bronco, your private yacht, your floating retreat, your speeding surfboard! It is a hollow, airtight wood or fiberglass shell propelled by the wind against its single, simply rigged colorful sail and is steered by a detachable rudder.

WHERE?

You may enjoy your Sailfish on any body of water three feet deep or over. A river, lake, even protected ocean areas are suitable for your boating ventures. Since the boat is light (100 lbs. for Sailfish; 139 lbs. for Sunfish) it is easily carried by two people, will fit on the top of a car, in a standard station wagon or it may be hauled on a trailer for overland transport. The Sailfisher may take his fun and excitement wherever he finds water. Your boat may be launched from a ramp or pier or simply placed in the water at the edge of the shore. No special facilities are necessary.

WHEN? Your heartiness against cold or windy conditions places the only limitation on when you can sail your Sailfish. Since the Sailfish is designed with no cockpit you will be partially wet most of the time. As a rule, when you would be comfortable swimming, you have ideal conditions for a trip on your Sailfish. The Sunfish has a small cockpit and since you stay comparatively dry in this boat, it can be sailed where and when the water is colder.

WHY? With a steady full wind holding a taut sail against the brilliant sky and you pointing toward a mark, you are indeed a king! You can sail simply for the exhilarating fun of it or you can teach your child or a "landlubber" the principles of an exciting sail. For complete relaxation or challenging competition you will be rewarded over every ripple of water.

SAILING ATTIRE

Unless you are an artful dodger and a skillful sailor, you will get wet on a Sailfish, and probably on a Sunfish, so a bathing suit is the uniform of the day with a blouse or sport shirt for protection from the sun. Sneakers without socks are helpful for protecting the feet if the launching area is rough. For sure-seating and comfort, many sailors wear padded sailing shorts. We also recommend U.S.C.G. approved life jackets, particularly for children. Now put some lotion on your nose and you are ready to go!

3
PREPARATION
for LAUNCHING

Preparing your boat for launching is simple and takes only a few minutes. It can be done in shallow water but is easier to do on shore with the boat on a launching dolly like "Big Sandy" shown above. "Big Sandy" is a lightweight dolly designed especially for carrying Sailfish and Sunfish over soft sand and rough terrain. You should have your sail already lashed to the two spars and one end of the halyard secured to the upper spar as indicated in the sail rigging instructions that come with your boat.* The mainsheet should be clipped to the bridle on the stern.

Following is a suggested list of steps:

1. Attach the rudder to the stern of the boat.
2. Lay the daggerboard on the deck near the slot in the center of the boat. Jam the board under the hand rails when you launch in the surf. In the Sunfish put the board in the cockpit.
3. Lay the sail and adjoining spars lengthwise on the port side of the deck so that the ring on the lower spar is over the mast hole.
4. Put the free end of the halyard through the pulley at the top of the mast and pull through four or five feet.
5. Place the bottom end of the mast through the ring on the lower boom and into the mast hole.
6. Be sure the drain plug is screwed in place.

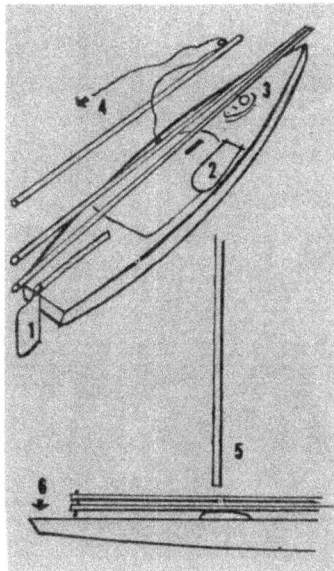

* *From now on when we refer to Sailfish, all comments apply to Sunfish as well.*

4

GETTING UNDERWAY

Walk your boat out to waist high water and put the daggerboard, straight edge forward, into the slot, pushing it all the way down. Point the bow of the boat toward the source of the wind and haul up the sail, securing the halyard to the cleat next to the mast hole. A look at a flag or waves will help you determine wind direction. Waves roll away from the wind's source. Shove off and jump aboard your craft slightly astern of center in the non-skid paint area of the deck. Hold the main sheet in one hand and the tiller in the other. Now fall off the wind. Pull in the sail until it fills and you will start speeding on your way.

HOW TO SAIL

Push the tiller to the right and left to get the feel of steering the boat. You will notice that it responds easily and is highly maneuverable. Now push the tiller one way or the other so that your boat is headed in the same direction that the waves are rolling or in the exact opposite direction from the source of the wind. This is called running before the wind.

A: *RUNNING:* Let the sail all the way out so that it is perpendicular to the boat. Sit amidships as the boat will not tip when running, unless the wind is strong and the waves high. In that case you must do the best balancing act you can. In our diagrams, X marks the spot where you should be sitting.

Running before the wind provides one of the greatest thrills in Sailfishing. You will skip over the waves at what seems like an incredible speed. If the wind is high and you catch a wave just right, your boat will plane like a surfboard and speeds up to 15 knots are possible.

FIG. 1 RUNNING
BEFORE THE WIND

Beware of letting the bow dip into a trough when you come off a wave. If the bow does go under, your momentum will start the boat submerging and pulling her out is not easy. (Leaning back helps.) If you go under too far, she will capsize most surely. But have no fear of tipping over, as righting the boat is easily accomplished. This is discussed fully under Capsizing.

When you are running, it is not advisable to have the wind coming directly from behind. Set your course so that the wind blows over the stern at a slight angle to

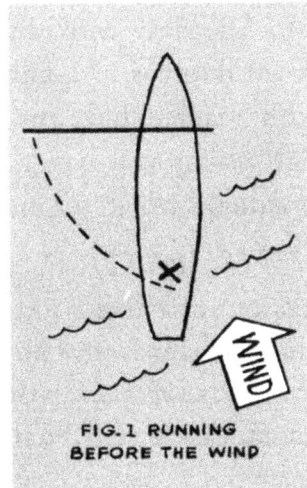

HOW TO SAIL

the line of the boat. (Fig. 1) If the wind comes over the starboard edge of the stern, put your sail out on the port side or vice-versa. This is to avoid an unnecessary jibe.

B. *REACHING:* Continuing as above, running with the sail out on the port side, push the tiller toward the sail until the wind is perpendicular to your boat. You are now reaching. (Fig. 2) Pull the sail in until it stops luffing and bring your tiller back to center. If the breeze is fair, the boat will heel a little, so you will want to sit on the windward side.

You have turned approximately 90 degrees in going from a run to a reach. Had you turned only half as far you would be on what is called a broad reach.

FIG. 2 REACHING

C. *BEATING:* Push the tiller toward the sail again until the wind comes over the starboard bow at a 45° angle. Pull in your sail at the same time as far as it will come. You have turned 45° and are sailing as close to the source of the wind as you can (Fig. 3) If the wind starts to tip the boat, let out the sail a bit to spill some of the wind or turn the boat into the wind a little. Both tactics will have a leveling or righting effect on your boat.

FIG. 3 BEATING

D. *COMING ABOUT:* Let us assume that you now wish to turn further in the same direction. Push the tiller toward the sail again. (Fig. 4a) Your bow will come into the wind as you turn, with the result that your sail will move to center and luff. (Fig. 4b) Keep the tiller over and hold on to the sheet. After you have turned far enough, the sail will shift to the other side and fill again. (Be sure your head is lower than the boom when it swings!) Bring the tiller to center and your boat will resume forward speed. (Fig. 4c)

You have just come about. Naturally you cannot sail directly to a point from which the wind is blowing. You have to come about back and forth across the wind to get there, changing your position on the boat each time as indicated on the diagrams with the X.

Before you made the turn into the wind above, you were beating with the wind coming over the starboard bow. You were, therefore, on the starboard tack. After you turned, the wind came over the port bow, so you changed to the port tack.

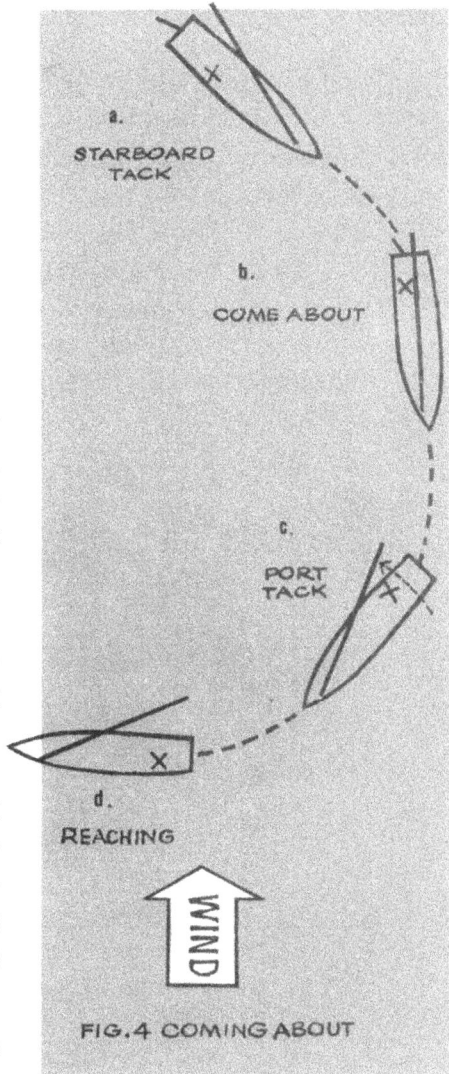

a.
STARBOARD
TACK

b.
COME ABOUT

c.
PORT
TACK

d.
REACHING

WIND

FIG.4 COMING ABOUT

HOW TO SAIL

Your Sailfish loses almost all its momentum when it comes about. It turns on the proverbial dime, but unless you execute this turn sharply, your boat may not make the turn completely. You will have no way on and the bow will be pointing directly into the wind. Nautically speaking, you will be "in irons". Ways out of this predicament are described in the section "Capsizing".

Now let's keep turning in the same direction—this time away from the wind's source. After you have turned 90° from the wind you will be reaching again. (Fig. 4d) Then as you keep turning, you will come back to running. You should be letting your sail out as you turn. On any course always let the sail out as far as it will go without luffing.

E. *JIBING:* As you continue to turn, the wind will come over your stern (Fig. 5a) When the boat is directly in line with the wind, pull in the sail and keep turning. The wind will catch the back of the sail and flop it over to the other side of the boat. (Fig. 5b) Caution—when you jibe, keep full slack available in the sheet but maintain control with a firm grip on the end of the sheet. Following the jibe, haul in on the sheet and come to a steady course. As in coming about, you should shift your weight during the jibe to the opposite side of the boat.

You have now sailed around the compass. (Fig. 1 to Fig. 5)

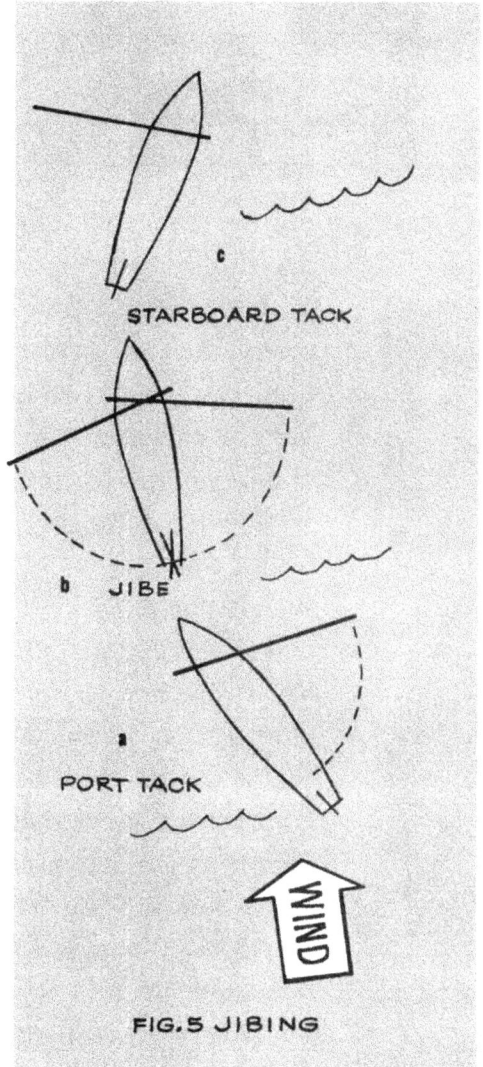

STARBOARD TACK

b JIBE

PORT TACK

WIND

FIG.5 JIBING

6 CAPSIZING

As a practiced sailor you may very well survive an entire season without overturning into the drink. If you are either less experienced or more adventurous, you will probably take a few spills, but be assured that nothing more than time is lost. A quick gust of wind or a difficult jibe may send your boat flying over, but your boat will be just where you left it and easy to get under way again. While you are in the water, push your boat to a position so that the bow is pointing into the wind. Simply stand or put your full weight on the daggerboard until the boat swings upright; climb aboard and regain your main sheet and tiller. You are now "in irons"—i.e., not moving at all since your boat is headed directly into the wind. In a few moments the wind will push the boat backwards. Since the action of the rudder is just opposite when you are backing up, push the tiller in the direction you wish to turn rather than away from that direction as you would when going forward. When you have fallen off the wind and gained a little forward speed, bring the tiller back to center.*

Every newcomer to the Sailfish should practice capsizing so that when it occurs as an accident he will be prepared to handle this situation. Because the Sunfish has a wider beam it is less likely to capsize, however, should it go over, it is no more difficult to right because the daggerboard is longer.

*To fall off more quickly, pull up the daggerboard halfway and pull in the boom by hand, holding overhead until the sail fills.

Though the process of righting your boat will never be too difficult, unless the wind is unusually strong, it may be tiring after a long sail. Adults as well as children will be more than happy to be wearing some kind of life belt as mentioned, so that energies may be devoted to the task rather than to staying afloat. No matter what difficulties you may encounter, ALWAYS STAY WITH YOUR BOAT. This is, of course, a fundamental water safety rule but particularly important with Sailfish and Sunfish which may foster a casual attitude. *Your boat will not sink*—see that you don't.

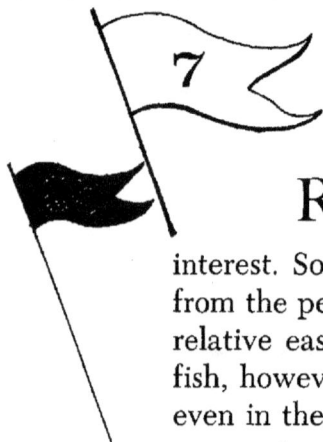

RACING

For many a Sailfish enthusiast, racing is of little interest. Some may prefer to "Sunday Sail" and benefit from the peace and glory of the outdoors. Because of the relative ease of holding a race between Sailfish or Sunfish, however, such contests are the high point of sailing even in these tiny boats. We have found that many non-racers stand aside when the warning gun sounds, not entirely from preference, but more often from lack of confidence and hesitation to compete with sailors who appear to know all the angles of the sailor's trade. As in most sports, this fear of competition is quickly changed to a surging enthusiasm after but a few experiences. GET

OUT AND RACE! That's the way to learn to employ your knowledge of maneuvers, turning, beating, etc., and turn them into tactics that may someday put you in first place across the finish. Racing will naturally improve your sailing too, simply by giving you a chance to observe other boats and sailors at close hand, who are in relatively the same circumstances as you. You may learn to handle your boat just a bit more precisely when you are forced to point a little higher or even take an opposite tack to beat a close rival!

Although a 14-year old is lighter than his father, the latter may be a better tactician so one never really knows who will win. To have your child beat you when you

know you tried your best is a memory that is not soon forgotten by father or child.

A good way for a racing novice who has mastered his turns and tacks might be to join one or two other boats on a short race to a single point and back home. This way, the racer who is learning is not so plagued with a great number of boats jockeying in and out; he can concentrate on the best handling of his own boat and still compare the performance of his boat with others. Every treatise, long or short on this subject, promotes as its cardinal rule, "Sail your own boat". In most instances, this advice is correct but we feel that beginners cannot help but learn from watching as well as doing.

In a lake-type area of water, any number of boats may race a course successfully providing the start and finish lines are adequate. The basic course is triangular, to permit all three tacks, a reach, a run and a beat. Any order or combination of tacks is permissible but a windward start is recommended for these reasons: 1. Boats are separated more in the beginning, making less congestion. 2. Less traffic accumulates about the first marker. It must be recognized, however, that this is the most difficult leg so beginning sailors may prefer to sail it last, giving each sailor a greater chance for a change of position up until the finish of the race.

RACING  TACTICS

STARTING: Assuming you have a windward start, your first question is—"where is the best place on the line for me to start?" Here is one way to help you decide. Sail your boat to the middle of the starting line and turn it directly into the wind. (Fig. 1). Then, determine whether your bow is pointing more in the direction of the starting flag on your port side or the one to starboard. In Fig. 1, your bow is pointing more toward the flag to port or the western end of the line. This tells you that the western end is favored; it is the higher or *windward* end and, therefore, closer to the first marker.

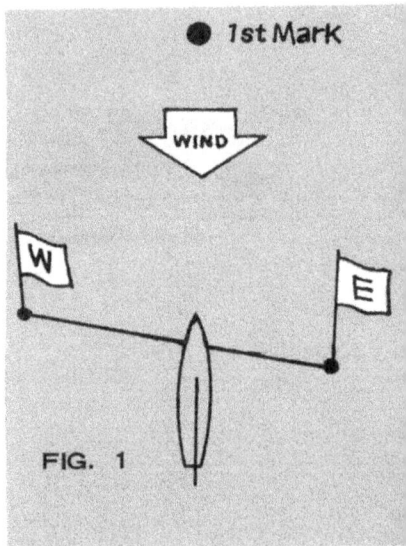

Race committees will generally lay the line 5 to 10 degrees off from perpendicular to the wind's source, so that it *does* favor the end shown in Fig. 1. But don't as-

sume this. Always test the line yourself as explained above. A late wind shift after the line has been laid can favor the other end of the line.

Assuming the western end is favored as in Fig. 1, the next step is to decide which tack to take. If you start on port (Fig. 2—Boat A), you should be sure that you will be able to cross over the bows of the boats starting at other places on the line on starboard tack. Those boats will have right of way over you, so if you cannot clear their bows, you will have to give way and come about, putting you to leeward of them. It is difficult, of course, to be sure of clearing them until just before the starting gun when you can see where the other boats are starting. (There always seems to be at least one boat that will start on starboard tack at the western end—Fig. 3 boat B—who makes it impossible for you to get away clear.)

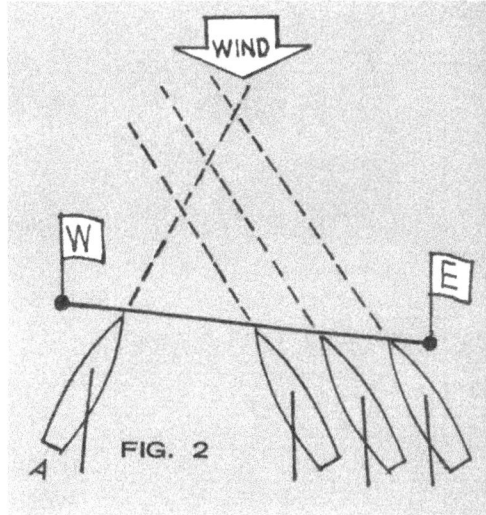

FIG. 2

Therefore, starting on port tack is risky and is to be avoided as a general rule. Occasionally you may find yourself alone at the western end. This would be the only time to gamble a start on port.

When the line is set as it is in Figs. 2 and 3, you will make a good start by approaching the line on starboard tack as Boat B is doing.

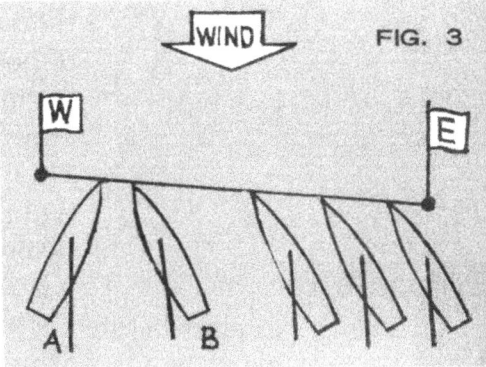

FIG. 3

You will have the advantage of being on the favored end with right of way to boot.

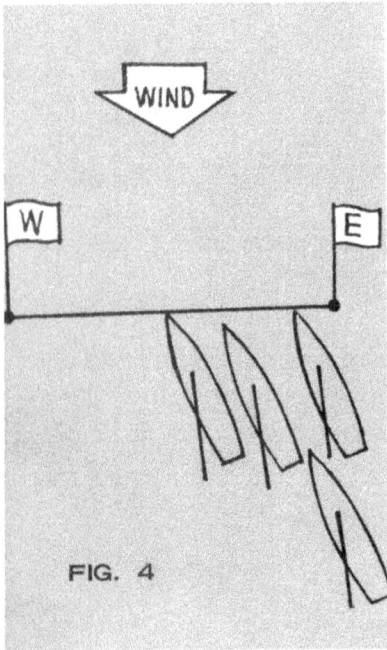

FIG. 4

If, when testing the line to determine the better end, you find that the western end has no particular advantage, *or* that the eastern end is favored, starting on starboard tack at the eastern end is your best bet. However, in this case, it is likely that many others will have the same idea resulting in a great cluster of boats at the eastern end (Fig. 4). For a beginner, it is wiser not to get in the crowd. *The most important thing in starting is to get into the free air,* so your boat will move. If there is a traffic jam at the favored end, start in the middle or elsewhere. Be flexible. Decide where you want to start before the race, but if too many have the same place in mind, find a clear spot on the line and start there.

If you are a more experienced sailor, and starting on starboard tack at the eastern end is favored, you will probably want to take your chances with the crowd. Set your last run for the line (Fig. 5—Boat A) so that you are close-hauled and your course will take you just inside the eastern flag; then you will have right of way over everyone to windward. If some of the other boats like C and D try to squeeze in, they are barging and must give way to you.

In many races, someone will get to line early and luff or run down the line to stall for time. You can force this boat over the line, if you are close hauled and coming up to the line on starboard tack on a converging course.

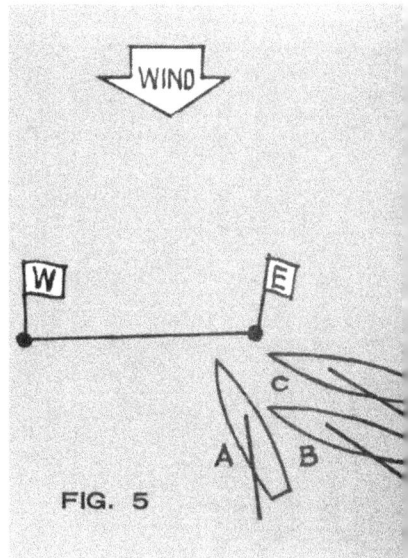

FIG. 5

Getting to the Line at the Starting Gun is Imperative!
If you are not there when the gun goes, the odds are great that one or more of the other boats will block off the free air and blanket you. Use a stop watch or wrist watch with a sweep second hand.

As a suggestion for getting there on time—when you have figured out where you want to start on the line, get your boat to that spot two minutes before the gun. Then sail the boat behind the line along the reverse of the course you will take back to the line (Fig. 6), Come about after 1 minute, and then go for the line full speed. You should hit it within a few seconds of the gun.

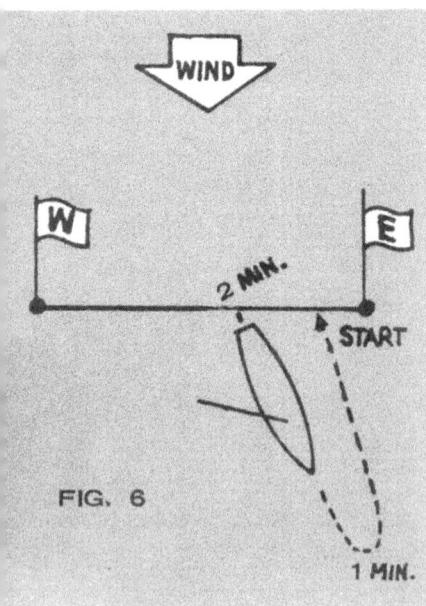

FIG. 6

TACKING: Immediately after starting check to see that you are not being blanketed by another boat. Also, be sure you are not sailing directly behind someone. The backwind will slow you down. If you are in either position, come about right away and get into the free air (Fig. 7—Boat A).

Sit as close to the center of the boat as you can on the windward side, and lean out as necessary to keep the boat almost flat. Heeling is exciting but slows you down in racing. Sailfish and Sunfish move fastest when they are almost flat. (In a light breeze you may want to put a little weight on the leeward side to give the *little* heel you need.)

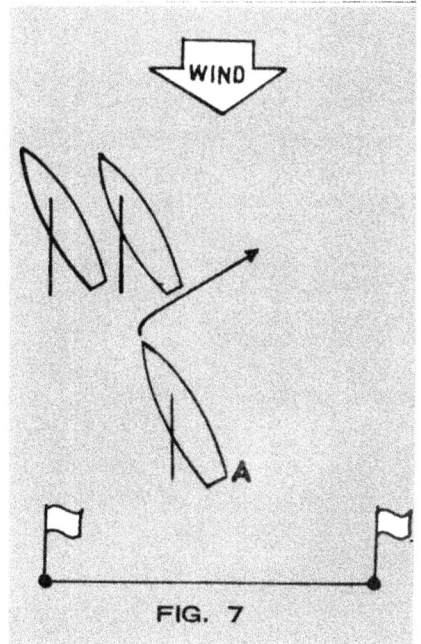

FIG. 7

Once in the clear, your next questions are—"which tacks should be taken and when?" Keep in mind that it is better to take as few tacks as possible, because coming about costs about two boat lengths per turn. Determine first which tack will take you closer to the marker. (In Fig. 8 tack or course B is closer.) Then, when a line from the

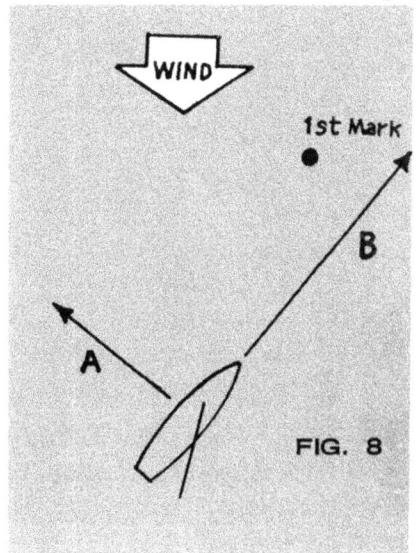

FIG. 8

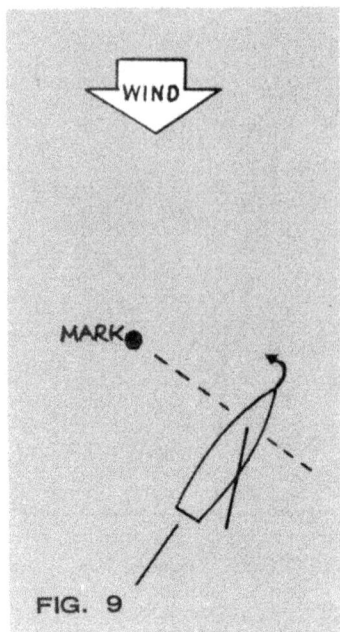

FIG. 9

marker to your boat is perpendicular to the fore and aft line of the boat, go 20 or 30 yards farther and come about (Fig. 9). You should be able to "lay" or get around the marker now.

The idea in taking the tack that is closer to the marker is simply to make it easier for you to tell when you can lay it—and to avoid losing ground from going too far on the first tack (overstaying the mark).

It is not always possible or wise to make the first marker on just two tacks. In the first place, you may be sailing along course B and another boat will come toward you on starboard tack. To keep clear you may have to come about. He has the right of way. Secondly, you should always be alert to shifts in the wind, and if it changes as indicated in Fig. 10 from North to Northwest, you will be unfavorably "headed" by staying on course B. Test the heading for 15 to 30 seconds to see if it is reasonably permanent, and if so, come about. Now you are on another course from your plan but one that will gain ground for you, because the shift in wind favors this tack. In our experience, the winning skippers are those who constantly watch for wind shifts and take advantage of them.

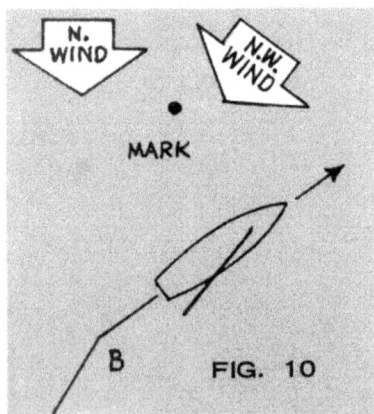

FIG. 10

Further, in planning your tacks after the start, the tack closer to the mark may result in your being on port tack after you have come about to lay the mark (Fig. 11). It is always advisable to approach the mark on starboard tack so you will have right of way and not have to alter your course for anyone. In this case come about a little earlier than you would to lay the mark. Then, come about again and go into the mark on starboard tack (dotted line—Fig. 11).

Still another occasion when you may not make the first marker on two tacks is when you are the lead boat. After the start you are proceeding along the tack of your choice, but if the second boat takes the other tack, you will probably want to cover her— to do everything she does so you will always be between her and the next marker. This could result in a dozen tacks as she tries to get clear of you.

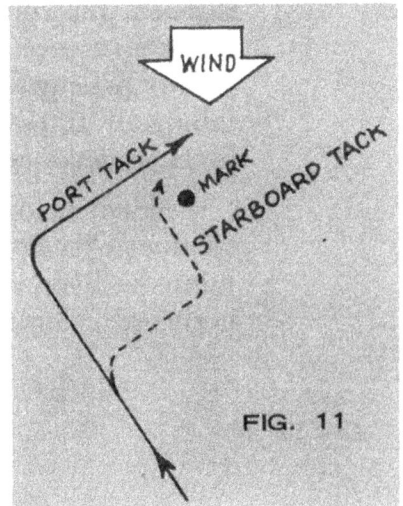

FIG. 11

Finally, you may be the second boat. One way to get ahead is to tack back and forth behind the lead boat coming about on headings. You have the advantage of tacking when you want to. The headings may not be as favorable for the lead boat when she comes about to cover you.

One of the most important aspects of tacking is pointing your boat well. Pull the sail in to a point where the lower boom hangs over the corner of the stern—not any farther in or you will be pinching the sail. Then, point the boat as close to the wind as you can (until the sail luffs slightly). Bear off a little to keep the sail full. The wind changes direction constantly, and because most changes are imperceptible, you should be always working your tiller—pointing the boat up until the little luff appears and then bearing off, over and over again. Be particularly alert to puffs, because they will usually allow you to point higher.

REACHING AND RUNNING: Assuming the second leg is a reach, head directly for the next marker and get your boat moving as fast as possible. Some skippers pull up the daggerboard halfway to decrease water resistance. If there are boats immediately in front of you try passing them by heading up to windward and then falling off. If they are anticipating your move by sailing up high, go down under them to leeward.

When running keep the daggerboard up (unless the weather is heavy) and sit back a little. On occasion in a light wind you can further benefit from pulling the daggerboard completely out. It is all right to sail a straight

line course to the next mark, but some skippers like to go down to leeward a little, so they can reach up to the mark near the end of the leg. The boat moves a little faster on a broad reach than on a run. Use the same tactics to pass other boats as in reaching above.

When approaching a mark from a broad reach **or run,** stay about a boat length away from the mark until you turn. Then, as you turn, come in close to the mark on the leeward side of it. Sailing close to the mark *before* the turn makes it difficult to stay close just after the turn. More than likely you will make an arc allowing any boat behind you to slip in between you and the marker (Fig. 12).

Finally, it is easy to lose the mainsheet when running. Be sure to knot the free end so it will not run back through the pulley on the lower boom.

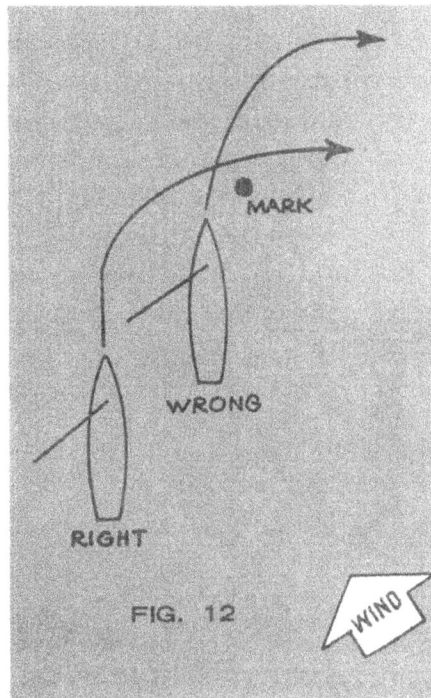

FIG. 12

8 RULES

Every game has rules and Sailfish-Sunfish racing is no exception, but because the boats are simpler in design and rigging and sailed in small bodies of water, some special rules apply. We follow the North American Yacht Racing Rules but with certain adaptations for our boats and group. The following digest of the rules is presented only as a guide for the convenience of Sailfish and Sunfish groups who wish to sail by generally accepted racing rules.

1. At the starting line, a leeward boat close hauled need not give way to a windward boat running free at an angle to the normal starting course. The windward boat is barging.

2. Boats returning from a premature start have no rights.

3. On the port tack a boat must keep clear of all starboard tack boats, except in two special situations, namely; (a) when, with the wind aft, she approaches a mark of the course and comes between that mark and a boat on the starboard tack; and (b) when the boat on the starboard tack is on the wrong side of the starting line at the signal and is returning to start.

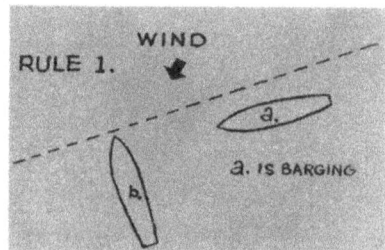

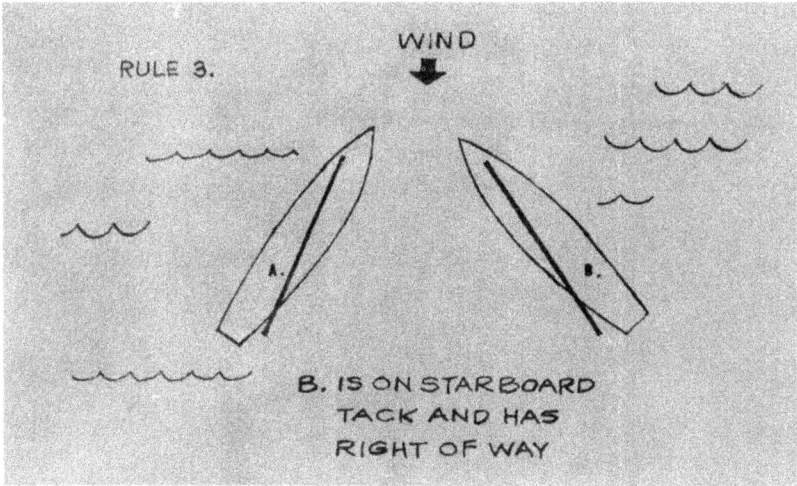

RULE 3.

WIND

B. IS ON STARBOARD
TACK AND HAS
RIGHT OF WAY

4. The windward of two boats on the same tack must keep clear and may not bear off on the leeward boat to prevent her from passing.

5. A leeward boat may luff a windward or overtaking boat until the windward boat reaches a point where the end of the tiller, excluding the extension is abeam of the leeward boat's mast — "mast abeam"; thereafter the leeward boat must return to her proper course.

6. Overtaking boats must keep clear.

RULES 4. & 5.

WIND

A.

B.

B. IS LEEWARD BOAT
AND HAS RIGHT OF WAY

RULES

7. Boats tacking or jibing must keep clear of boats on a tack. If tacking or jibing simultaneously, the boat to port keeps clear.

8 A right-of-way boat must not balk or alter course when the other is in the act of keeping clear or unable to respond.

9. Boats can hail for room to tack to clear an obstruction but must tack as soon as room is given.

10. An outside boat must give room at turning marks and obstructions to overlapping boats on the same tack, and at leeward marks to boats on the same or opposite tacks, regardless of their relative courses. In case of doubt whether an overlap was established in time, assume it was not.

9 MAINTENANCE

Always hose down your boat and sail with fresh water after sailing in salt water. Leave the sail hanging off the ground as shown in the illustration. Coil the main sheet and halyard and tie them to one of the spars, so they will not drag on the ground and be subject to rot.

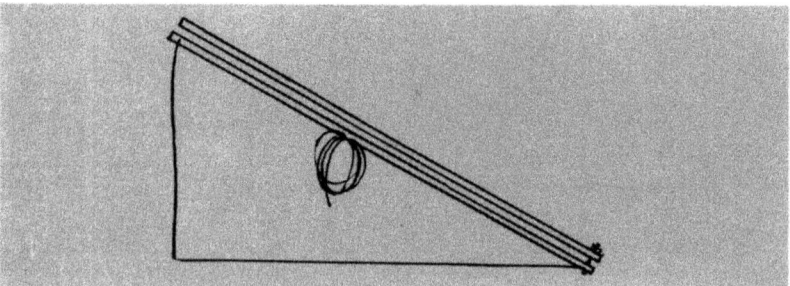

10 STORAGE

A Sailfish or Sunfish can be stored in your garage without taking up much room. Although, as we pointed out, the boats can be transported easily, it is most convenient to store them at the sailing site. If you have a boat club or water front house, storing the boats on shelves in sheds works out well. With rollers on the shelves, the boats will slide in and out easily.

HAPPY SAILING!

We hope this book will lead you to discovering the fun of Sailfishing. There are more advanced and more specific books on small boat sailing and racing that we urge you to read as your interest in sailing develops. Our objective has been to provide you with the basic essentials of sailing and an adaptation of sailing principles to the Sailfish and the Sunfish.

GLOSSARY

AMIDSHIPS—center area of boat

BOW—forward part of boat

CAPSIZE—to overturn

CLOVE HITCH—sailor's knot used to attach halyard to upper boom

COME ABOUT—turning boat so that bow passes across source of wind

DAGGERBOARD—wooden piece that fits into slot on Sailfish and Sunfish to keep boat from slipping sideways — sometimes called a centerboard

DRAIN PLUG—plug on boat used for draining water out of boat

FALL OFF THE WIND—to turn the bow away from the source of the wind

HALYARD—rope line used for raising sail

HEEL—to tip or list

JIBE—when running before the wind, to bring the sail from one side to the other

LUFFING—flapping of the sail when it is pointed into the wind

MAIN SHEET—rope used to pull in or let out sail

MARKER—stationary buoy used for races

GLOSSARY

MAST—vertical spar that supports upper boom, lower
      boom and sail

PORT SIDE—left side of boat looking forward

RUDDER—wooden piece fastened to stern used in con-
      junction with tiller to steer boat

SPARS—long wooden or aluminum booms to which sail
      is attached

STARBOARD—right side of boat looking forward

STERN—back of boat

TACK—a sailing course

TILLER—long piece of wood that fits into the head of the
      rudder and is used to steer the boat

WAY—forward movement

WINDWARD—toward the wind. Windward side of boat
      is closest to source of wind—leeward,
      away from wind

We hope you enjoyed this title from Echo Point Books & Media

Before Closing this Book, Two Good Things to Know

1. Buy Direct & Save

Go to www.echopointbooks.com (click "Our Titles" at top or click "For Echo Point Publishing" in the middle) to see our complete list of titles. We publish books on a wide variety of topics—from spirituality to auto repair.

Buy direct and save 10% at www.echopointbooks.com

DISCOUNT CODE: EPBUYER

2. Make Literary History and Earn $100 Plus Other Goodies Simply for Your Book Recommendation!

At Echo Point Books & Media we specialize in republishing out-of-print books that are united by one essential ingredient: high quality. Do you know of any great books that are no longer actively published? If so, please let us know. If we end up publishing your recommendation, you'll be adding a wee bit to literary culture and a bunch to our publishing efforts.

Here is how we will thank you:

- A free copy of the new version of your beloved book that includes acknowledgement of your skill as a sharp book scout.

- A free copy of another Echo Point title you like from echopointbooks.com.

- And, oh yes, we'll also send you a check for $100.

Since we publish an eclectic list of titles, we're interested in a wide range of books. So please don't be shy if you have obscure tastes or like books with a practical focus. To get a sense of what kind of books we publish, visit us at www.echopointbooks.com.

If you have a book that you think will work for us,
send us an email at editorial@echopointbooks.com

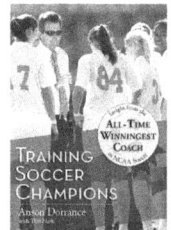

www.ingramcontent.com/pod-product-compliance
Lightning Source LLC
Chambersburg PA
CBHW061003050426
42453CB00009B/1232